MW00509207

AIR FRYER
EASY RECIPES

The Best Way to Eat Light and Stay Fit

STEVE GOLEN

© **Copyright 2021 - All rights reserved.**

The content contained within this book may not be reproduced, duplicated or transmitted without direct written permission from the author or the publisher.

Under no circumstances will any blame or legal responsibility be held against the publisher, or author, for any damages, reparation, or monetary loss due to the information contained within this book. Either directly or indirectly.

Legal Notice:

This book is copyright protected. This book is only for personal use. You cannot amend, distribute, sell, use, quote or paraphrase any part, or the content within this book, without the consent of the author or publisher.

Disclaimer Notice:

Please note the information contained within this document is for educational and entertainment purposes only. All effort has been executed to present accurate, up to date, and reliable, complete information. No warranties of any kind are declared or implied. Readers acknowledge that the author is not engaging in the rendering of legal, financial, medical or professional advice. The content within this book has been derived from various sources. Please consult a licensed professional before attempting any techniques outlined in this book.

By reading this document, the reader agrees that under no circumstances is the author responsible for any losses, direct or indirect, which are incurred as a result of the use of information contained within this document, including, but not limited to, errors, omissions, or inaccuracies.

STEVE GOLEN

Table of Contents

Introduction

What is an air fryer?

Is an appliance that typically has an egg shape, more or less square, with a removable basket on which you put the food to be cooked. It takes advantage of the concept of air cooking at high temperatures that reach up to 200 ° allowing a healthy "frying-not-frying" of fresh foods. Abandon, then, the thought of frying during which the food is immersed in a lot of oil because the number of oil used inside the air fryer could be as little as a couple of teaspoons of spray. True frying in plenty of boiling oil is almost as "dangerous", especially in case you abuse it or don't pay proper attention. In the air fryer, the oil never reaches the smoke point and is therefore non-toxic.

Hot air, which reaches high temperatures, circulates inside the chamber of the air fryer allowing the food to be cooked evenly both externally and internally. This way you will cook meat, fish, vegetables, and thousands of other dishes in no time - in short, you can make many recipes with the air fryer. Meat cooked in an air fryer is juicy, tender, and soft, excess fat drips down and does not remain inside the meat giving it exceptional flavor.

The air fryer also works as an oven and grill...

The air fryer is quite different and in addition to its main purpose, the air cooking of food for a light and healthy fried food, it is also an appliance that serves as an oven for gratin for different recipes, pasta dishes, vegetables, to cook cakes and pies of all kinds, muffins, buns, pizzas. It has been shown that in the best performing models, the air fryer eliminates excess fat, even up to 50%, without altering the flavor of foods, giving the right crispness typical of fried foods.

Which air fryer to choose to buy?

For the choice of air fryer, the advice could also be an honest product to solicit better and better results. A high-quality product returns a product of equal quality. It would therefore be fair to consider spending slightly more for a much better-performing air fryer that also has better quality materials. However, depending on your needs, there are now many excellent products that are affordable for everyone.

Now you simply need to take a look inside the air fryer recipes. They are all proven, safe and excellent recipes!

Country Pie with Walnuts

Ingredients
1 cup coconut milk

2 eggs

1/2 stick butter, at room temperature

1 teaspoon vanilla essence

1/4 teaspoon ground cardamom

1/4 teaspoon ground cloves

1/2 cup walnuts, ground

1/2 cup sugar

1/3 cup almond flour

Directions
Begin by preheating your Air Fryer to 360 degrees F. Spritz the sides and bottom of a baking pan with nonstick cooking spray.

Mix all ingredients until well combined. Scrape the batter into the prepared baking pan.

Bake approximately 13 minutes; use a toothpick to test for doneness. Bon appétit!

Per serving: 244 Calories; 19.1g Fat; 12.7g Carbs; 6.5g Protein; 10.9g Sugars

Chocolate and Peanut Butter Brownies

Ingredients
1 cup peanut butter
1 ¼ cups sugar
3 eggs
1 cup all-purpose flour
1 teaspoon baking powder
1/4 teaspoon kosher salt
1 cup dark chocolate, broken into chunks

Directions
Start by preheating your Air Fryer to 350 degrees F. Now, spritz the sides and bottom of a baking pan with cooking spray.
In a mixing dish, thoroughly combine the peanut butter with the sugar until creamy. Next, fold in the egg and beat until fluffy.
After that, stir in the flour, baking powder, salt, and chocolate. Mix until everything is well combined.
Bake in the preheated Air Fryer for 20 to 22 minutes. Transfer to a wire rack to cool before slicing and serving. Bon appétit!

Per serving: 291 Calories; 7.9g Fat; 48.2g Carbs; 6.4g Protein; 32.3g Sugars

Cocktail Party Fruit Kabobs

Ingredients

2 pears, diced into bite-sized chunks

2 apples, diced into bite-sized chunks

2 mangos, diced into bite-sized chunks

1 tablespoon fresh lemon juice

1 teaspoon vanilla essence

2 tablespoons maple syrup

1 teaspoon ground cinnamon

1/2 teaspoon ground cloves

Directions

Toss all ingredients in a mixing dish.

Tread the fruit pieces on skewers.

Cook at 350 degrees F for 5 minutes. Bon appétit

Per serving: 165 Calories; 0.7g Fat; 41.8g Carbs; 1.6g Protein; 33.6g Sugars

Classic Vanilla Mini Cheesecakes

Ingredients

1/2 cup almond flour

1 ½ tablespoons unsalted butter, melted

1 tablespoon white sugar

1 (8-ounce) package cream cheese, softened

1/4 cup powdered sugar

1/2 teaspoon vanilla paste 1 egg, at room temperature

Topping:

1 ½ cups sour cream

3 tablespoons white sugar

1 teaspoon vanilla extract

1/4 cup maraschino cherries

Directions

Thoroughly combine the almond flour, butter, and sugar in a mixing bowl. Press the mixture into the bottom of lightly greased custard cups.

Then, mix the cream cheese, 1/4 cup of powdered sugar, vanilla, and egg using an electric mixer on low speed. Pour the batter into the pan, covering the crust.

Bake in the preheated Air Fryer at 330 degrees F for 35 minutes until edges are puffed and the surface is firm.

Mix the sour cream, 3 tablespoons of white sugar, and vanilla for the topping; spread over the crust and allow it to cool to room temperature.

Transfer to your refrigerator for 6 to 8 hours. Decorate with maraschino cherries and serve well chilled.

Per serving: 321 Calories; 25g Fat; 17.1g Carbs; 8.1g Protein; 11.4g Sugars

Green Pea Fritters with Parsley Yogurt Dip

Ingredients

Pea Fritters:

1 ½ cups frozen green peas

1 tablespoon sesame oil

1/2 cup scallions, chopped

2 garlic cloves, minced

1 cup chickpea flour

1 teaspoon baking powder

1/2 teaspoon sea salt

1/2 teaspoon ground black pepper

1/4 teaspoon dried dill

1/2 teaspoon dried basil

Parsley Yogurt Dip:

1/2 cup Greek-Style yoghurt

2 tablespoons mayonnaise

2 tablespoons fresh parsley, chopped

1 tablespoon fresh lemon juice

1/2 teaspoon garlic, smashed

Directions

Place the thawed green peas in a mixing dish; pour in hot water. Drain and rinse well. Mash the green peas; add the remaining ingredients for the pea fritters and mix to combine well. Shape the mixture into patties and transfer them to the lightly greased cooking basket.

Bake at 330 degrees F for 14 minutes or until thoroughly heated. Meanwhile, make your dipping sauce by whisking the remaining ingredients. Place in your refrigerator until ready to serve.

Serve the green pea fritters with the chilled dip on the side. Enjoy!

Per serving: 233 Calories; 11.3g Fat; 23.8g Carbs; 9.4g Protein; 6.9g Sugars

Homemade Pork Scratchings

Ingredients

1 pound pork rind raw, scored by the butcher

1 tablespoon sea salt

2 tablespoon smoked paprika

Directions

Sprinkle and rub salt on the skin side of the pork rind. Allow it to sit for 30 minutes.

Roast at 380 degrees F for 8 minutes; turn them over and cook for a further 8 minutes or until blistered.

Sprinkle the smoked paprika all over the pork scratchings and serve. Bon appétit!

Per serving: 245 Calories; 14.1g Fat; 0g Carbs; 27.6g Protein; 0g Sugars

German Blueberry Dessert with Pecan Streusel

Ingredients

2 cups fresh blueberries

1 teaspoon fresh lemon juice

1/4 teaspoon lemon zest

1/2 teaspoon crystallized ginger

2 ounces brown sugar

1/2 cup pecans, chopped

2 tablespoons honey

1/2 teaspoon ground cinnamon

2 tablespoons cold salted butter, cut into pieces

Directions

Place the fresh blueberries on the bottom of a lightly buttered Air Fryer-safe dish.

In a mixing bowl, thoroughly combine the remaining ingredients for the topping.

Top your blueberries with the prepared topping.

Bake your dessert at 340 degrees F for about 17 minutes. Serve at room temperature and enjoy!

Per serving: 331 Calories; 17.3g Fat; 47.5g Carbs; 2.3g Protein; 40.5g Sugars

Cranberry Cornbread Muffins

Ingredients

3/4 cup all-purpose flour
3/4 cup cornmeal
1 teaspoon baking powder
1/2 teaspoon baking soda
1/2 teaspoon salt
3 tablespoons honey
1 egg, well whisked
1/4 cup olive oil
3/4 cup milk
1/2 cup fresh cranberries, roughly chopped

Directions

In a mixing dish, thoroughly combine the flour, cornmeal, baking powder, baking soda, and salt. In a separate bowl, mix the honey, egg, olive oil, and milk.

Next, stir the liquid mixture into the dry ingredients; mix to combine well. Fold in the fresh cranberries and stir to combine well.

Pour the batter into a lightly greased muffin tin; cover with aluminum foil and poke tiny little holes all over the foil. Now, bake for 15 minutes.

Remove the foil and bake for 10 minutes more. Transfer to a wire rack to cool slightly before cutting and serving. Bon appétit!

Per serving: 439 Calories; 18.2g Fat; 60.9g Carbs; 8.2g Protein; 19.7g Sugars

Rosemary Roasted Mixed Nuts

Ingredients

1 tablespoons butter, at room temperature

1 tablespoon dried rosemary

1 teaspoon coarse sea salt

1/2 teaspoon paprika

1/2 cup pine nuts

1 cup pecans

1/2 cup hazelnuts

Directions

Toss all the ingredients in the mixing bowl.

Line the Air Fryer basket with baking parchment. Spread out the coated nuts in a single layer in the basket.

Roast at 350 degrees F for 6 to 8 minutes, shaking the basket once or twice. Work in batches. Enjoy!

Per serving: 295 Calories; 30.2g Fat; 5.8g Carbs; 4.8g Protein; 1.6g Sugars

Cheese and Garlic Stuffed Chicken Breasts

Ingredients
1/2 cup Cottage cheese
1 eggs, beaten
2 medium-sized chicken breasts, halved
2 tablespoons fresh coriander, chopped
1teaspoon fine sea salt
Seasoned breadcrumbs
1/3teaspoon freshly ground black pepper, to savor
2 cloves garlic, finely minced

Directions
Firstly, flatten out the chicken breast using a meat tenderizer.
In a medium-sized mixing dish, combine the Cottage cheese with the garlic, coriander, salt, and black pepper.
Spread 1/3 of the mixture over the first chicken breast. Repeat with the remaining ingredients. Roll the chicken around the filling; make sure to secure with toothpicks.
Now, whisk the egg in a shallow bowl. In another shallow bowl, combine the salt, ground black pepper, and seasoned breadcrumbs.
Coat the chicken breasts with the whisked egg; now, roll them in the breadcrumbs.
Cook in the air fryer cooking basket at 365 degrees F for 22 minutes.
Serve immediately.

Per serving: 424 Calories; 24.5g Fat; 7.5g Carbs; 43.4g Protein; 5.3g Sugars

Farmer's Breakfast Deviled Eggs

Ingredients

6 eggs

6 slices bacon

2 tablespoons mayonnaise

1 teaspoon hot sauce

1/2 teaspoon Worcestershire sauce

2 tablespoons green onions, chopped

1 tablespoon pickle relish

Salt and ground black pepper, to taste

1 teaspoon smoked paprika

Directions

Place the wire rack in the Air Fryer basket; lower the eggs onto the wire rack.

Cook at 270 degrees F for 15 minutes.

Transfer them to an ice-cold water bath to stop the cooking. Peel the eggs under cold running water; slice them into halves.

Cook the bacon at 400 degrees F for 3 minutes; flip the bacon over and cook an additional 3 minutes; chop the bacon and reserve.

Mash the egg yolks with the mayo, hot sauce, Worcestershire sauce, green onions, pickle relish, salt, and black pepper; add the reserved bacon and spoon the yolk mixture into the egg whites.

Garnish with smoked paprika. Bon appétit!

Per serving: 512 Calories; 42.9g Fat; 5.1g Carbs; 25.2g Protein; 3.6g Sugars

Colby Potato Patties

Ingredients

1 pounds white potatoes, peeled and grated

1/2 cup scallions, finely chopped

1/2 teaspoon freshly ground black pepper, or more to taste

1 tablespoon fine sea salt

1/2 teaspoon hot paprika

2 cups Colby cheese, shredded

1/4 cup canola oil

1 cup crushed crackers

Directions

Firstly, boil the potatoes until fork tender. Drain, peel and mash your potatoes.

Thoroughly mix the mashed potatoes with scallions, pepper, salt, paprika, and cheese. Then, shape the balls using your hands. Now, flatten the balls to make the patties.

In a shallow bowl, mix canola oil with crushed crackers. Roll the patties over the crumb mixture.

Next, cook your patties at 360 degrees F approximately 10 minutes, working in batches. Serve with tabasco mayo if desired. Bon appétit!

Per serving: 291 Calories; 18.0g Fat; 23.7g Carbs; 9.3g Protein; 1.7g Sugars

Baked Eggs Florentine

Ingredients
1 tablespoon ghee, melted
2 cups baby spinach, torn into small pieces
2 tablespoons shallots, chopped
1/4 teaspoon red pepper flakes
Salt, to taste
1 tablespoon fresh thyme leaves, roughly chopped
4 eggs

Directions
Start by preheating your Air Fryer to 350 degrees F. Brush the sides and bottom of a gratin dish with the melted ghee.
Put the spinach and shallots into the bottom of the gratin dish. Season with red pepper, salt, and fresh thyme.
Make four indents for the eggs; crack one egg into each indent. Bake for 12 minutes, rotating the pan once or twice to ensure even cooking. Enjoy!

Per serving: 325 Calories; 25.1g Fat; 5.1g Carbs; 19.1g Protein; 2.2g Sugars

Mother's Day Pudding

Ingredients

1 pound French baguette bread, cubed

4 eggs, beaten

1/4 cup chocolate liqueur

1 cup granulated sugar

2 tablespoons honey

2 cups whole milk

1/2 cup heavy cream

1 teaspoon vanilla extract

1/4 teaspoon ground cloves

2 ounces milk chocolate chips

Directions

Place the bread cubes in a lightly greased baking dish. In a mixing bowl, thoroughly combine the eggs, chocolate liqueur, sugar, honey, milk, heavy cream, vanilla, and ground cloves.

Pour the custard over the bread cubes. Scatter the milk chocolate chips over the top of your bread pudding.

Let stand for 30 minutes, occasionally pressing with a wide spatula to submerge.

Cook in the preheated Air Fryer at 370 degrees F degrees for 7 minutes; check to ensure even cooking and cook an additional 5 to 6 minutes. Bon appétit!

Per serving: 548 Calories; 11.8g Fat; 92.2g Carbs; 14.9g Protein; 57.4g Sugars

Easy Fried Button Mushrooms

Ingredients
1 pound button mushrooms
1 cup cornstarch
1 cup all-purpose flour
1/2 teaspoon baking powder
2 eggs, whisked
2 cups seasoned breadcrumbs
1/2 teaspoon salt
2 tablespoons fresh parsley leaves, roughly chopped

Directions
Pat the mushrooms dry with a paper towel.
To begin, set up your breading station. Mix the cornstarch, flour, and baking powder in a shallow dish. In a separate dish, whisk the eggs.
Finally, place your breadcrumbs and salt in a third dish.
Start by dredging the mushrooms in the flour mixture; then, dip them into the eggs. Press your mushrooms into the breadcrumbs, coating evenly.
Spritz the Air Fryer basket with cooking oil. Add the mushrooms and cook at 400 degrees F for 6 minutes, flipping them halfway through the cooking time.
Serve garnished with fresh parsley leaves. Bon appétit!

Per serving: 259 Calories; 4.3g Fat; 47.5g Carbs; 8.7g Protein; 2.4g Sugars

Classic Egg Salad

Ingredients

6 eggs
1 teaspoon mustard
1/2 cup mayonnaise
1 tablespoons white vinegar
2 carrots, trimmed and sliced
1 red bell pepper, seeded and sliced
1 green bell pepper, seeded and sliced
1 shallot, sliced
Sea salt and ground black pepper, to taste

Directions

Place the wire rack in the Air Fryer basket; lower the eggs onto the wire rack.

Cook at 270 degrees F for 15 minutes.

Transfer them to an ice-cold water bath to stop the cooking. Peel the eggs under cold running water; coarsely chop the hard-boiled eggs and set aside.

Toss with the remaining ingredients and serve well chilled. Bon appétit!

Per serving: 294 Calories; 21.2g Fat; 10.5g Carbs; 14.9g Protein; 4.9g Sugars

Cajun Turkey Meatloaf

Ingredients

1 1/3 pounds turkey breasts, ground

½ cup vegetable stock

2 eggs, lightly beaten

1/2 sprig thyme, chopped

1/2 teaspoon Cajun seasonings

1/2 sprig coriander, chopped

½ cup seasoned breadcrumbs

2 tablespoons butter, room temperature

1/2 cup scallions, chopped

1/3 teaspoon ground nutmeg

1/3 cup tomato ketchup

1/2 teaspoon table salt

2 teaspoons whole grain mustard

1/3 teaspoon mixed peppercorns, freshly cracked

Directions

Firstly, warm the butter in a medium-sized saucepan that is placed over a moderate heat; sauté the scallions together with the chopped thyme and coriander leaves until just tender.

While the scallions are sautéing, set your air fryer to cook at 365 degrees F.

Combine all the ingredients, minus the ketchup, in a mixing dish; fold in the sautéed mixture and mix again.

Shape into a meatloaf and top with the tomato ketchup. Air-fry for 50 minutes. Bon appétit!

Per serving: 429 Calories; 31.6g Fat; 8.3g Carbs; 25.3g Protein; 2.2g Sugars

Veggie Casserole with Ham and Baked Eggs

Ingredients
2 tablespoons butter, melted
1 zucchini, diced
1 bell pepper, seeded and sliced
1 red chili pepper, seeded and minced
1 medium-sized leek, sliced
3/4 pound ham, cooked and diced
5 eggs
1 teaspoon cayenne pepper
Sea salt, to taste
1/2 teaspoon ground black pepper
1 tablespoon fresh cilantro, chopped

Directions
Start by preheating the Air Fryer to 380 degrees F. Grease the sides and bottom of a baking pan with the melted butter.
Place the zucchini, peppers, leeks and ham in the baking pan. Bake in the preheated Air Fryer for 6 minutes.
Crack the eggs on top of ham and vegetables; season with the cayenne pepper, salt, and black pepper. Bake for a further 20 minutes or until the whites are completely set.
Garnish with fresh cilantro and serve. Bon appétit!

Per serving: 325 Calories; 20.9g Fat; 7.9g Carbs; 26.6g Protein; 2.8g Sugars

Dinner Turkey Sandwiches

Ingredients

1/2 pound turkey breast

1 teaspoon garlic powder

7 ounces condensed cream of onion soup

1/3 teaspoon ground allspice

BBQ sauce, to savor

Directions

Simply dump the cream of onion soup and turkey breast into your crock-pot. Cook on HIGH heat setting for 3 hours.

Then, shred the meat and transfer to a lightly greased baking dish. Pour in your favorite BBQ sauce. Sprinkle with ground allspice and garlic powder. Air-fry an additional 28 minutes.

To finish, assemble the sandwiches; add toppings such as pickled or fresh salad, mustard, etc.

Per serving: 114 Calories; 5.6g Fat; 3.6g Carbs; 13.1g Protein; 0.2g Sugars

Tender Beef Chuck with Brussels Sprouts

Ingredients

1 pound beef chuck shoulder steak

2 tablespoons vegetable oil

1 tablespoon red wine vinegar

1 teaspoon fine sea salt

1/2 teaspoon ground black pepper

1 teaspoon smoked paprika

1 teaspoon onion powder

1/2 teaspoon garlic powder

1/2 pound Brussels sprouts, cleaned and halved

1/2 teaspoon fennel seeds

1 teaspoon dried basil

1 teaspoon dried sage

Directions

Firstly, marinate the beef with vegetable oil, wine vinegar, salt, black pepper, paprika, onion powder, and garlic powder. Rub the marinade into the meat and let it stay at least for 3 hours. Air fry at 390 degrees F for 10 minutes. Pause the machine and add the prepared Brussels sprouts; sprinkle them with fennel seeds, basil, and sage. Turn the machine to 380 degrees F; press the power button and cook for 5 more minutes. Pause the machine, stir and cook for further 10 minutes. Next, remove the meat from the cooking basket and cook the vegetables a few minutes more if needed and according to your taste. Serve with your favorite mayo sauce.

Per serving: 302 Calories; 14.2g Fat; 6.5g Carbs; 36.6g Protein; 1.6g Sugars

Easy Roasted Hot Dogs

Ingredients
6 hot dogs
6 hot dog buns
1 tablespoon mustard
6 tablespoons ketchup
6 lettuce leaves

Directions
Place the hot dogs in the lightly greased Air Fryer basket.
Bake at 380 degrees F for 15 minutes, turning them over halfway
through the cooking time to promote even cooking.
Place on the bun and add the mustard, ketchup, and lettuce leaves.
Enjoy!

**Per serving: 415 Calories; 15.2g Fat; 41.4g Carbs; 28.1g Protein;
11.8g Sugars**

Famous Western Eggs

Ingredients

6 eggs
3/4 cup milk
1 ounce cream cheese, softened
Sea salt, to your liking
1/4 teaspoon ground black pepper
1/4 teaspoon paprika
6 ounces cooked ham, diced
1 onion, chopped
1/3 cup cheddar cheese, shredded

Directions

Begin by preheating the Air Fryer to 360 degrees F. Spritz the sides and bottom of a baking pan with cooking oil.

In a mixing dish, whisk the eggs, milk, and cream cheese until pale. Add the spices, ham, and onion; stir until everything is well incorporated.

Pour the mixture into the baking pan; top with the cheddar cheese. Bake in the preheated Air Fryer for 12 minutes. Serve warm and enjoy!

Per serving: 336 Calories; 22.6g Fat; 7.2g Carbs; 25.1g Protein; 4.7g Sugars

Beef and Kale Omelet

Ingredients
Non-stick cooking spray
1/2 pound leftover beef, coarsely chopped
2 garlic cloves, pressed
1 cup kale, torn into pieces and wilted
1 tomato, chopped
1/4 teaspoon brown sugar
4 eggs, beaten
4 tablespoons heavy cream
1/2 teaspoon turmeric powder
Salt and ground black pepper, to your liking
1/8 teaspoon ground allspice

Directions
Spritz the inside of four ramekins with a cooking spray.
Divide all of the above ingredients among the prepared ramekins.
Stir until everything is well combined.
Air-fry at 360 degrees F for 16 minutes; check with a wooden stick
and return the eggs to the Air Fryer for a few more minutes as
needed. Serve immediately.

**Per serving: 236 Calories; 13.7g Fat; 4.0g Carbs; 23.8g Protein;
1.0g Sugars**

Mozzarella Stick Nachos

Ingredients

1 (16-ounce) package mozzarella cheese sticks

2 eggs

1/2 cup flour

1/2 (7 12-ounce) bag multigrain tortilla chips, crushed

1 teaspoon garlic powder

1 teaspoon dried oregano

1/2 cup salsa, preferably homemade

Directions

Set up your breading station. Put the flour into a shallow bowl; beat the eggs in another shallow bowl; in a third bowl, mix the crushed tortilla chips, garlic powder, and oregano.

Coat the mozzarella sticks lightly with flour, followed by the egg, and then the tortilla chips mixture. Place in your freezer for 30 minutes.

Place the breaded cheese sticks in the lightly greased Air Fryer basket. Cook at 380 degrees F for 6 minutes.

Serve with salsa on the side and enjoy!

Per serving: 551 Calories; 28.7g Fat; 36.3g Carbs; 39.1g Protein; 1.7g Sugars

Sweet Mini Monkey Rolls

Ingredients

3/4 cup brown sugar

1 stick butter, melted

1/4 cup granulated sugar

1 teaspoon ground cinnamon

1/4 teaspoon ground cardamom

1 (16-ounce) can refrigerated buttermilk biscuit dough

Directions

Spritz 6 standard-size muffin cups with nonstick spray. Mix the brown sugar and butter; divide the mixture between muffin cups. Mix the granulated sugar with cinnamon and cardamom. Separate the dough into 16 biscuits; cut each in 6 pieces. Roll the pieces over the cinnamon sugar mixture to coat. Divide between muffin cups. Bake at 340 degrees F for about 20 minutes or until golden brown. Turn upside down and serve.

Per serving: 446 Calories; 23.7g Fat; 54.1g Carbs; 5.3g Protein; 22.5g Sugars

Cajun Fish Cakes with Cheese

Ingredients
2 catfish fillets
1 cup all-purpose flour
3 ounces butter
1 teaspoon baking powder
1 teaspoon baking soda
1/2 cup buttermilk
1 teaspoon Cajun seasoning
1 cup Swiss cheese, shredded

Directions
Bring a pot of salted water to a boil. Boil the fish fillets for 5 minutes or until it is opaque. Flake the fish into small pieces.
Mix the remaining ingredients in a bowl; add the fish and mix until well combined. Shape the fish mixture into 12 patties.
Cook in the preheated Air Fryer at 380 degrees F for 15 minutes. Work in batches. Enjoy!

Per serving: 478 Calories; 30.1g Fat; 27.2g Carbs; 23.8g Protein; 2g Sugars

Double Cheese Fish Casserole

Ingredients

1 tablespoon avocado oil

1 pound hake fillets

1teaspoon garlic powder

Sea salt and ground white pepper, to taste

2 tablespoons shallots, chopped

1 bell pepper, seeded and chopped

1/2 cup Cottage cheese

1/2 cup sour cream

1 egg, well whisked

1 teaspoon yellow mustard

1 tablespoon lime juice

1/2 cup Swiss cheese, shredded

Directions

Brush the bottom and sides of a casserole dish with avocado oil.
Add the hake fillets to the casserole dish and sprinkle with garlic powder, salt, and pepper.

Add the chopped shallots and bell peppers.

In a mixing bowl, thoroughly combine the Cottage cheese, sour cream, egg, mustard, and lime juice. Pour the mixture over fish and spread evenly.

Cook in the preheated Air Fryer at 370 degrees F for 10 minutes.
Top with the Swiss cheese and cook an additional 7 minutes. Let it rest for 10 minutes before slicing and serving. Bon appétit!

Per serving: 456 Calories; 30.1g Fat; 8.8g Carbs; 36.7g Protein; 3g Sugars

Turkey Meatballs

Ingredients

½ pounds ground turkey

1/2 cup parmesan cheese, grated 1/2 cup tortilla chips, crumbled 1 yellow onion, finely chopped

2 tablespoons Italian parsley, finely chopped 1 egg, beaten

2 cloves garlic, minced 1 tablespoon soy sauce

1 teaspoon Italian seasoning mix 1 teaspoon olive oil

Directions:

Thoroughly combine all of the above ingredients until well incorporated. Shape the mixture into 10 equal meatballs.

Spritz a cooking basket with a nonstick cooking spray. Cook at 360 degrees F for about 10 minutes or to your desired degree of doneness.

Per serving: 327 Calories; 18.7g Fat; 6.9g Carbs; 32.2g Protein; 1.7g Sugars

Chicken Drumettes with Peppers

Ingredients

1/2 cup all-purpose four 1 teaspoon kosher salt1 teaspoon shallot powder
1/2 teaspoon dried basil 1/2 teaspoon dried oregano
1/2 teaspoon smoked paprika 1 tablespoon hot sauce
1/4 cup mayonnaise 1/4 cup milk
1 pound chicken drumettes 2 bell peppers, sliced

Directions

In a shallow bowl, mix the flour, salt, shallot powder, basil, oregano and smoked paprika. In another bowl, mix the hot sauce, mayonnaise and milk.

Dip the chicken drumettes in the flour mixture, then, coat them with the milk mixture; make sure to coat well on all sides.

Cook in the preheated Air Fryer at 380 degrees F for 28 to 30 minutes; turn them over halfway through the cooking time. Reserve chicken drumettes, keeping them warm.

Then, cook the peppers at 400 degrees F for 13 to 15 minutes, shaking the basket once or twice. Eat warm.

Per serving: 397 Calories; 18.8g Fat; 20.6g Carbs; 34.2g Protein; 3.1g Sugars

Pork Loin and Roasted Peppers

Ingredients

3 red bell peppers
1 ½ pounds pork loin 1 garlic clove, halved
1 teaspoon lard, melted
1/2 teaspoon cayenne pepper 1/4 teaspoon cumin powder 1/4 teaspoon
ground bay laurel
Kosher salt and ground black pepper, to taste

Directions

Roast the peppers in the preheated Air Fryer at 395 degrees F for 10
minutes, flipping them halfway through the cooking time.
Let them steam for 10 minutes; then, peel the skin and discard the
stems and seeds. Slice the peppers into halves and add salt to taste.
Rub the pork with garlic; brush with melted lard and season with spices
until well coated on all sides.
Place in the cooking basket and cook at 360 digress F for 25 minutes.
Turn the meat over and cook an additional 20 minutes. Serve with
roasted peppers.

**Per serving: 409 Calories; 20.1g Fat; 4.3g Carbs; 49g Protein; 2.4g
Sugars**

Barbecue meatloaf muffins

Ingredients

1 pound lean ground pork 1 small onion, chopped
2 cloves garlic, crushed 1/4 cup carrots, grated
1 serrano pepper, seeded and minced 1 teaspoon stone-ground mustard 1/4
cup crackers, crushed
1 egg, lightly beaten
Sea salt and ground black pepper, to taste 1/2 cup BBQ sauce

Directions

Mix all ingredients, except for the BBQ sauce, until everything is well
incorporated.
Brush a muffin tin with vegetable oil. Use an ice cream scoop to spoon the
meat mixture into the cups. Top each meatloaf cup with a spoonful of BBQ
sauce.
Bake in the preheated Air Fryer at 395 degrees F for about 40 minutes.
Transfer to a cooling rack.
Wait for a few minutes before unmolding and serving.

**Per serving: 269 Calories; 9.7g Fat; 9.1g Carbs; 36.6g Protein; 4.4g
Sugars**

Steak with honey butter

Ingredients

1 pound flank steak 1/2 teaspoon olive oil
Sea salt and red pepper flakes, to taste 3 tablespoons butter
1 teaspoon Dijon mustard 1 teaspoon honey

Directions

Brush the flank steak with olive oil and season with salt and pepper.
Cook at 400 degrees F for 6 minutes. Then, turn the steak halfway
through the cooking time and continue to cook for a further 6 minutes.
In the meantime, prepare the Dijon honey butter by whisking the
remaining ingredients. Serve the warm flank steak dolloped with the
Dijon honey butter.

**Per serving: 333 Calories; 19.8g Fat; 3.5g Carbs; 32.8g Protein;
3.1g Sugars**

Simple burgers

Ingredients

3/4 pound lean ground chuck
Kosher salt and ground black pepper, to taste 3 tablespoons onion, minced
1 teaspoon garlic, minced 1 teaspoon soy sauce
1/2 teaspoon smoked paprika 1/4 teaspoon ground cumin 1/2 teaspoon
cayenne pepper 1/2 teaspoon mustard seeds 2 burger buns

Directions

Thoroughly combine the ground chuck, salt, black pepper, onion,
garlic and soy sauce in a mixing dish.
Season with smoked paprika, ground cumin, cayenne pepper and
mustard seeds. Mix to combine well.
Shape the mixture into 2 equal patties.
Spritz your patties with a nonstick cooking spray. Air fry your burgers
at 380 degrees F for about 11 minutes or to your desired degree of
doneness.
Place your burgers on burger buns and serve with favorite toppings.
Devour!

**Per serving: 433 Calories; 17.4g Fat; 40g Carbs; 39.2g Protein; 6.4g
Sugars**

Salad with beans, cheese and almonds

Ingredients

1 ½ pounds green beans, trimmed and cut into small chunks Sea salt and
ground black pepper, to taste
1 small-sized red onion, sliced
2 bell peppers, deseeded and sliced 1/2 cup goat cheese, crumbled
1/4 cup almonds Dressing:
1 tablespoon champagne vinegar 1 tablespoon Shoyu sauce
2 tablespoons extra-virgin olive oil 1 teaspoon deli mustard
1 clove garlic, pressed

Directions

Season the green beans with salt and black pepper to your liking. Brush
them with a nonstick cooking oil.

Place the green beans in the Air Fryer cooking basket. Cook the green
beans at 400 degrees F for 5 minutes and transfer to a salad bowl. Stir
in the onion and bell peppers.

Then, add the raw almonds to the cooking basket. Roast the almonds
at 350 degrees F for 5 minutes, shaking the basket periodically to
ensure even cooking.

In the meantime, make the dressing by blending all ingredients until
well incorporated. Dress your salad and top with goat cheese and
roasted almonds.

**Per serving: 290 Calories; 17.3g Fat; 25.6g Carbs; 13.8g Protein;
11.5g Sugars**

Roasted asparagus and Roman cheese

Ingredients

1 pound asparagus spears, trimmed 1 teaspoon sesame oil

1/2 teaspoon garlic powder 1/2 teaspoon shallot powder 1/4 teaspoon cumin powder 1/2 teaspoon dried rosemary

Coarse sea salt and ground black pepper, to taste 4 tablespoons Pecorino Romano cheese, grated 1 tablespoon sesame seeds, toasted

Directions

Start by preheating your Air Fryer to 400 degrees F.

Toss your asparagus with sesame oil, spices and cheese and transfer to the Air Fryer cooking basket.

Cook your asparagus in the preheated Air Fryer for 5 to 6 minutes, shaking the basket halfway through the cooking time to ensure even browning.

Garnish with toasted sesame seeds and serve warm.

Per serving: 109 Calories; 5.9g Fat; 8.5g Carbs; 7.8g Protein; 3.7g Sugars

Mexican crunchy cheese sticks

Ingredients

1/2 cup almond flour

1/4 teaspoon xanthan gum 1/4 teaspoon shallot powder 1/4 teaspoon garlic powder 1/4 teaspoon ground cumin 1 egg yolk, whisked

1 ounce Manchego cheese, grated 2 ounces Cotija cheese, grated

Directions

Mix all ingredients until everything is well incorporated.

Twist the batter into straw strips and place them on a baking mat inside your Air Fryer.

Cook the cheese straws in your Air Fryer at 360 degrees F for 5 minutes; turn them over and cook an additional 5 minutes.

Let the cheese straws cool before serving.

Per serving: 138 Calories; 11g Fat; 0.8g Carbs; 7.8g Protein; 0.2g Sugars

Greek zucchini

Ingredients

1/2 pound zucchini, cut into thin rounds 1 teaspoon extra-virgin olive oil
1/2 teaspoon dried sage, crushed 1/2 teaspoon oregano
1/4 teaspoon ground bay leaf
Coarse sea salt and ground black pepper, to taste Greek dipping sauce:
1/2 cup Greek yogurt
1/2 teaspoon fresh lemon juice 2 tablespoons mayonnaise
1/2 teaspoon garlic, pressed

Directions

Toss the zucchini rounds with olive oil and spices and place them in the Air Fryer cooking basket.

Cook in the preheated Air Fryer at 400 degrees F for 10 minutes; shaking the basket halfway through the cooking time.

Let it cool slightly and cook an additional minute or so until crispy and golden brown.

Meanwhile, make the sauce by whisking all the sauce ingredients; place the sauce in the refrigerator until ready to serve.

Serve the crispy zucchini rounds with Greek dipping sauce on the side.

Per serving: 128 Calories; 1.2g Fat; 6.2g Carbs; 3.9g Protein; 2.7g Sugars

Chocolate cake

Ingredients

1/2 cup self-rising flour

6 tablespoons brown sugar 5 tablespoons coconut milk 4 tablespoons coconut oil

4 tablespoons unsweetened cocoa powder 2 eggs

A pinch of grated nutmeg A pinch of salt

Directions

Mix all the ingredients together; divide the batter between two mugs. Place the mugs in the Air Fryer cooking basket and cook at 390 degrees F for about 10 minutes.

Per serving: 546 Calories; 34.1g Fat; 55.4g Carbs; 11.4g Protein; 25.7g Sugars

Turkey Thighs

Ingredients

1 tablespoon sesame oil

2 pounds turkey thighs

1 teaspoon Chinese Five-spice powder

1 teaspoon pink Himalayan salt

1/4 teaspoon Sichuan pepper

6 tablespoons honey

1 tablespoon Chinese rice vinegar

2 tablespoons soy sauce

1 tablespoon sweet chili sauce

1 tablespoon mustard

Directions

Preheat your Air Fryer to 360 degrees F.

Brush the sesame oil all over the turkey thighs. Season them with spices.

Cook for 23 minutes, turning over once or twice. Make sure to work in batches to ensure even cooking

In the meantime, combine the remaining ingredients in a wok (or similar type pan) that is preheated over medium-high heat. Cook and stir until the sauce reduces by about a third.

Add the fried turkey thighs to the wok; gently stir to coat with the sauce.

Let the turkey rest for 10 minutes before slicing and serving.

Per serving: 279 Calories; 10.1g Fat; 19g Carbs; 27.7g Protein; 17.9g Sugars

Chicken Wings Flavored With Garlic Butter

Ingredients
1 pound chicken wings
Salt and black pepper, to taste
1 tablespoons butter
1 teaspoon garlic paste
1 lemon, cut into slices

Directions
Pat dry the chicken wings with a kitchen towel and season all over with salt and black pepper.
In a bowl, mix together butter and garlic paste. Rub the mixture all over the wings.
Cook in the preheated Air Fryer at 380 degrees F for 18 minutes.
Serve garnished with lemon slices.

Per serving: 270 Calories; 13.1g Fat; 2.9g Carbs; 33.6g Protein; 1.5g Sugars

Burgers Turkey with Vermouth and Bacon

Ingredients

1 tablespoons vermouth

1 tablespoon honey

2 strips Canadian bacon, sliced

1 pound ground turkey

1/2 shallot, minced

2 garlic cloves, minced

2 tablespoons fish sauce

Sea salt and ground black pepper, to taste

1 teaspoon red pepper flakes

4 soft hamburger rolls

4 tablespoons tomato ketchup

4 tablespoons mayonnaise

4 (1-ounce) slices Cheddar cheese

4 lettuce leaves

Directions

Start by preheating your Air Fryer to 400 degrees F.
Whisk the vermouth and honey in a mixing bowl; brush the
Canadian bacon with the vermouth mixture. Cook for 3 minutes.
Flip the bacon over and cook an additional 3 minutes. Then,
thoroughly combine the ground turkey, shallots, garlic, fish sauce,
salt, black pepper, and red pepper. Form the meat mixture into 4
burger patties. Bake in the preheated Air Fryer at 370 degrees F for
10 minutes. Flip them over and cook another 10 minutes.
Spread the ketchup and mayonnaise on the inside of the hamburger
rolls and place the burgers on the rolls; top with bacon, cheese and
lettuce; serve immediately

**Per serving: 564 Calories; 30.6g Fat; 32.9g Carbs; 37.7g Protein;
11.1g Sugars**

Smoked Sausage and Sauerkraut

Ingredients

4 pork sausages, smoked

2 tablespoons canola oil

2 garlic cloves, minced

1 pound sauerkraut

1 teaspoon cayenne pepper

1/2 teaspoon black peppercorns

2 bay leaves

Directions

Start by preheating your Air Fryer to 360 degrees F.

Prick holes into the sausages using a fork and transfer them to the cooking basket. Cook approximately 14 minutes, shaking the basket a couple of times. Set aside.

Now, heat the canola oil in a baking pan at 380 degrees F. Add the garlic and cook for 1 minute. Immediately stir in the sauerkraut, cayenne pepper, peppercorns, and bay leaves.

Let it cook for 15 minutes, stirring every 5 minutes. Serve in individual bowls with warm sausages on the side!

Per serving: 478 Calories; 42.6g Fat; 6.1g Carbs; 17.2g Protein; 2.1g Sugars

Italian Piadina

Ingredients

1/2 pound ribeye steak

1 teaspoon sesame oil

Sea salt and red pepper, to taste

2 medium-sized piadinas

2 ounces Fontina cheese, grated

4 tablespoons Giardiniera

Directions

Brush the ribeye steak with sesame oil and season with salt and red pepper.

Cook at 400 degrees F for 6 minutes. Then, turn the steak halfway through the cooking time and continue to cook for a further 6 minutes.

Slice the ribeye steak into bite-sized strips. Top the piadinas with steak strips and cheese.

Heat the sandwich in your Air Fryer at 380 degrees F for about 3 minutes until the cheese melts. Top with Giardiniera and serve.

Per serving: 384 Calories; 24.8g Fat; 11.1g Carbs; 31.1g Protein; 4.9g Sugars

Barbecued Ribs

Ingredients

1 pound beef ribs

1/4 cup ketchup

1/4 cup tequila

1 tablespoon brown mustard

1 tablespoon brown sugar

2 tablespoons soy sauce1/2 red onion, sliced

2 garlic cloves, pressed

Directions

Cut the ribs into serving size portions and transfer them to a ceramic dish. Add in the remaining ingredients, cover and allow it to marinate in your refrigerator overnight.

Discard the marinade. Grill in the preheated Air Fryer at 400 degrees F for 10 minutes. Turn them over and continue to cook for 10 minutes more.

Meanwhile, make the sauce by warming the marinade ingredients in a nonstick pan. Spoon over the warm ribs and serve immediately

Per serving: 566 Calories; 45g Fat; 18g Carbs; 25.7g Protein; 10.3g Sugars

Catfish with Eggplant Sauce

Ingredients

1 pound catfish fillets
Sea salt and ground black pepper, to taste
1/4 cup Dijon mustard
1 tablespoon honey
1 tablespoon white vinegar
1 pound eggplant, 1 ½-inch cubes
2 tablespoons olive oil
1 tablespoon tahini
1/2 teaspoon garlic, minced
1 tablespoon parsley, chopped

Directions

Pat the catfish dry with paper towels and generously season with salt and black pepper.
In a small mixing bowl, thoroughly combine Dijon mustard, honey and vinegar.
Cook the fish in your Air Fryer at 400 degrees F for 5 minutes. Turn the fish over and brush with the Dijon mixture; continue to cook for a further 5 minutes.
Then, set your Air Fryer to 400 degrees F. Add the eggplant chunks to the cooking basket and cook for 15 minutes, shaking the basket occasionally to ensure even cooking.
Transfer the cooked eggplant to a bowl of your food processor; stir in the remaining ingredients and blitz until everything is well blended and smooth.
Serve the warm catfish with the eggplant sauce on the side.

Per serving: 336 Calories; 16.9g Fat; 18.6g Carbs; 28.2g Protein; 12.1g Sugars

Salmon with Cilantro Sauce

Ingredients
1 pound salmon fillets

1 teaspoon coconut oil

Sea salt and ground black pepper, to season

2 heaping tablespoons cilantro

1/2 cup Mexican crema

1 tablespoon fresh lime juice

Directions
Rinse and pat your salmon dry using paper towels. Toss the salmon with coconut oil, salt and black pepper.

Cook the salmon filets in your Air Fryer at 380 degrees F for 6 minutes; turn the salmon filets over and cook on the other side for 6 to 7 minutes.

Meanwhile, mix the remaining ingredients in your blender or food processor. Spoon the cilantro sauce over the salmon filets and serve immediately.

Per serving: 419 Calories; 20.2g Fat; 3.2g Carbs; 53.3g Protein; 1.6g Sugars

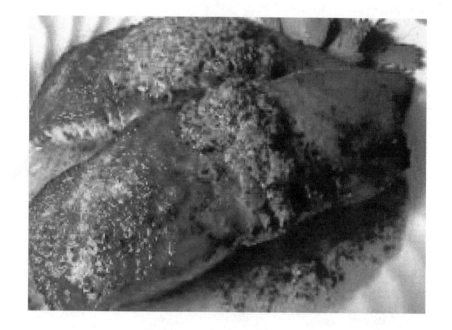

Prosciutto Stuffed Jalapeños

Ingredients

8 fresh jalapeño peppers, deseeded and cut in half lengthwise

4 ounces Ricotta cheese, at room temperature

1/4 teaspoon cayenne pepper

1/2 teaspoon granulated garlic

8 slices prosciutto, chopped

Directions

Place the fresh jalapeño peppers on a clean surface.

Mix the remaining ingredients in a bowl; divide the filling between the jalapeño peppers. Transfer the peppers to the Air Fryer cooking basket.

Cook the stuffed peppers at 400 degrees F for 15 minutes. Serve.

Per serving: 178 Calories; 8.7g Fat; 11.7g Carbs; 14.3g Protein; 4.6g Sugars

Pecorino Romano Meatballs

Ingredients

1/2 pound ground turkey

1 tablespoons tomato ketchup

1 teaspoon stone-ground mustard

2 tablespoons scallions, chopped

1 garlic clove, minced

1/4 Pecorino-Romano cheese, grated

1 egg, beaten

1/2 teaspoon red pepper flakes, crushed

Sea salt and ground black pepper, to taste

Directions

In a mixing bowl, thoroughly combine all ingredients.

Shape the mixture into 6 equal meatballs. Transfer the meatballs to the Air Fryer cooking basket that is previously greased with a nonstick cooking spray.

Cook the meatballs at 360 degrees F for 10 to 11 minutes, shaking the basket occasionally to ensure even cooking. An instant thermometer should read 165 degrees F.

Per serving: 264 Calories; 14.6g Fat; 3.7g Carbs; 29.7g Protein; 1.6g Sugars

Smoked Salmon and Rice Rollups

Ingredients
1 tablespoon fresh lemon juice

6 slices smoked salmon

1 tablespoon extra-virgin olive oil 1/2 cup cooked rice

1 tablespoon whole-grain mustard

3 tablespoons shallots, chopped

1 garlic clove, minced

1 teaspoon capers, rinsed and chopped

Sea salt and ground black pepper, to taste

3 ounces sour cream

Directions
Drizzle the lemon juice all over the smoked salmon.

Then, spread each salmon strip with olive oil. In a mixing bowl, thoroughly combine the cooked rice, mustard, shallots, garlic, and capers.

Spread the rice mixture over the olive oil. Roll the slices into individual rollups and secure with a toothpick. Season with salt and black pepper.

Place in the lightly greased Air Fryer basket. Bake at 370 degrees F for 16 minutes, turning them over halfway through the cooking time. Serve with sour cream.

Per serving: 226 Calories; 11.6g Fat; 15.1g Carbs; 15.2g Protein; 1.9g Sugars

Classic Donuts

Ingredients
8 ounces refrigerated buttermilk biscuits
2 tablespoons butter, unsalted and melted
1/2 tablespoon cinnamon
4 tablespoons caster sugar
A pinch of salt
A pinch of grated nutmeg

Directions
Separate the biscuits and cut holes out of the center of each biscuit using a 1-inch round biscuit cutter; place them on a parchment paper.
Lower your biscuits into the Air Fryer cooking basket. Brush them with 1 tablespoon of melted butter.
Air fry your biscuits at 340 degrees F for about 8 minutes or until golden brown, flipping them halfway through the cooking time.
Meanwhile, mix the sugar with cinnamon, salt and nutmeg.
Brush your donuts with remaining 1 tablespoon of melted butter; roll them in the cinnamonsugar and serve.

Per serving: 268 Calories; 12.2g Fat; 36.1g Carbs; 3.9g Protein; 12.4g Sugars